EVERYDAY GUIDES MADE EASY

USING YOUR
iPAD
BASICS

This is a **FLAME TREE** book
First published 2015

Publisher and Creative Director: Nick Wells
Project Editor: Laura Bulbeck
Art Director: Mike Spender
Layout Design: Jane Ashley
Copy Editor: Amanda Crook
Technical Editor: Mark Mayne
Screenshots: Roger Laing and Michael Sawh

Special thanks to: Polly Prior and Josie Mitchell

This edition first published 2015 by
FLAME TREE PUBLISHING
Crabtree Hall, Crabtree Lane
Fulham, London SW6 6TY
United Kingdom

www.flametreepublishing.com

15 17 19 18 16
1 3 5 7 9 10 8 6 4 2

© 2015 Flame Tree Publishing

ISBN 978-1-78361-399-1

A CIP record for this book is available from the British Library upon request.

Printed in China

All non-screenshot pictures are © 2015 Apple Inc.: 6, 7; and Shutterstock
and © the following photographers: Goodluz: 1, 63; Bloomua: 3, 10, 36, 56, 89, 90; Kudla:
5; Mihai Simonia: 8; manaemedia: 11, 14; Your Design: 13; Twin Design:
16, 21, 44, 51; YanLev: 18; Eugenio Marongiu: 28, 66, 70, 102; rangtheclick:
35; Bacho: 38, 64; Photodiem: 42; VGstockstudio: 47; imtmphoto: 49; Denphumi:
52; Denys Prykhodov: 58, 76; Jack Frog: 60, 83; Grzegorz Placzek: 68; blvdone:
73; Rocketclips, Inc.: 78; Syda Productions: 84, 94, 97, 101, 121; Neirfy:
85; 1000 Words: 98; Max Topchii: 108; baranq: 110; Sjale: 112; lightwavemedia:
116; BlueSkyImage: 118. All other images courtesy of Flame Tree Publishing Ltd.

EVERYDAY GUIDES
MADE EASY

USING YOUR
iPAD
BASICS

ROGER LAING & MICHAEL SAWH
SERIES FOREWORD BY MARK MAYNE

FLAME TREE
PUBLISHING

CONTENTS

Get started with this guide to setting up your iPad for the very first time.

Navigate your way around your iPad, and use the keyboard and voice dictation.

These step-by-step guides will have you surfing the net,
emailing and using maps in no time.

Discover how to find and download apps onto your iPad,
and then how to use them.

Your iPad is the perfect camera, video recorder and
music player – and is great for games.

Use your iPad for work, set up your calendar and contacts,
and ensure your work is secure.

SERIES FOREWORD

Since Apple launched the iPhone in 2007, and followed it up with the iPad in 2010, the consumer touchscreen technology sector has increased exponentially. There is now a bewildering variety of choices to make about the smartphone and tablet devices we carry with us, but this iPad Basics guide is here to help you navigate many of them.

Whether you're looking for entertainment, music, social connectivity, any business service you can think of, or a source of information about where you are and what you're looking at that very second, this iPad Basics guide will help you navigate the world of touchscreen tech and apps.

As with other titles in this series, we take a detailed look at the iPad, how to set it up and get the best out of it for your lifestyle, as well as how to get to grips with the basics of iOS, Apple's operating system. Don't worry, though – this guide is designed for absolute beginners, as well as those who are looking for more expert knowledge.

Finally, there's a comprehensive troubleshooting guide, full of the best tips and tricks to keep you and your device and operating system working in perfect harmony. Throughout each chapter there are Hot Tips to save you time and effort – keep a sharp look out!

This easy-to-use, step-by-step guide is written by a recognized expert in his field, so you can be sure of the best advice and the latest knowledge without breaking a sweat. The iPad Basics guide is an asset to any reference bookshelf – happy reading.

Mark Mayne Editor of T3.com

INTRODUCTION

Loved, desired and applauded since it was first launched, the iPad has revolutionized personal computing. Forget your laptop, the iPad is rapidly becoming the essential accessory for managing everyday life.

DIFFERENT GENERATIONS, SIMILAR FEATURES

Amazingly, since it first appeared in 2010, Apple has launched nine different models of iPad, each with two options available – Wi-Fi only and Wi-Fi plus Cellular. Unfortunately, the

naming of each model has been quite confusing. First there was the iPad followed by the iPad 2. Next came the third and fourth generation iPads before Apple renamed it the iPad Air. We shouldn't of course forget the smaller iPad Mini, which is now into its third generation.

Due to the fact that these different models support different hardware and different versions of Apple's iOS operating system, in this book we will mention where applicable whether the model does or does not support some of the newer features introduced by Apple.

Left: The iPad Air 2 has incredible screen clarity and is the fastest version yet.

iPAD'S OPERATING SYSTEM (iOS)

iOS is Apple's operating system for mobile devices such as the iPad, iPhone and the iPod Touch. iOS is regularly updated with new features.

The different versions of iOS

Each new version of iOS fixes some problems, such as security patches for Safari, as well as adding new features. Because some of these additions depend on a lot of processing power they are not available on all versions of the iPad. The latest version, iOS 8.1 is available on all iPad models apart from the first generation iPad.

SHORT SECTIONS

Pick up your iPad and flick through the screens and you'll often come across something new. Similarly, this book is not designed to be read in one sitting but to be a handy guide. For example, the section on gestures can be read on its own and you can practise them on your iPad until you feel confident that you can use them correctly. At the same time, it is a useful reference, if you need to remind yourself of some of the more advanced gestures later on.

STEP-BY-STEP

Throughout this book you'll find there are many step-by-step guides that take you through the precise actions you need to follow on certain tasks. This may be anything from connecting to your wireless network, setting up email or editing your photos to creating a new playlist for your music or troubleshooting app problems. Each step-by-step guide has clear, concise instructions on what to do and also explains any differences between the various iPad versions, so you can be sure you won't miss out.

Above: Screenshots accompany step-by-step instructions to take you through everything you need to know.

SETTING UP YOUR iPAD

ANATOMY OF AN iPAD

While there are few obvious physical differences between iPads, there are some subtle and not so subtle variations between each generation.

FRONT

❶ Headphone Socket
The 3.5 mm audio jack point works with the headphones you use with other Apple devices, such as the iPhone or iPod Touch.

❷ Sleep/Wake Button
Also known as the On/Off button.

- **Sleep mode**: Press this button once and this will put your iPad to sleep. To wake the iPad instantly, press the Sleep/Wake button again once (or the Home button) and swipe across the slide to unlock the screen.

- **Shutdown**: This turns the iPad off completely, saving your battery. To switch off, press and hold the Sleep/Wake button for a few seconds. Confirm your decision by using the slide to power off the button to shut down.

❸ FaceTime Camera
As its name suggests, this is mainly for use with FaceTime video chat, which we will go into more detail later on (see page 70).

Headphone socket ❶   FaceTime camera ❸   Sleep/wake button ❷

Display ❼

Home screen ❹

iPad dock ❺

❻ Home button

④ Home Screen

The Home screen hosts the app icons that you tap to run them. Swipe right on the Home screen and you'll flip through the different pages of apps you have available. You can also organize your apps into folders. To do so, just press on an app icon until it starts shaking and then drag it on top of the icon you want to share the folder. A folder is automatically created, which you can rename. Tap on the folder and you can access the apps inside.

Hot Tip

One way to preserve battery life is to set your screen to Auto-Lock when you're not using it. To do so, tap the Settings icon, select General, then Auto-Lock and set the interval to the time you prefer.

⑤ iPad Dock

This dock bar appears at the foot of the Home screen and stays in place as you scroll between the pages. It means these apps are always available from any Home screen page. You can customize the dock to include six apps of your choice. To add an app, press and hold until it begins to shake, then drag it to the dock. To make room for a different app, if you already have six in the dock, press and hold one of the apps and then drag it to the Home screen.

⑥ Home Button

This is the only physical button on the front of your iPad. When you are in one app, press this once to return to the main Home screen page and launch another app. Pressing it twice reveals the icons of apps that have recently been running.

- **Touch ID**: On the iPad Air 2 and the iPad Mini 3rd generation, this is where you will find the Touch ID biometric fingerprint sensor. This security feature can take a picture of up to five fingerprints and store them to be used to quickly unlock the iPad and authorize iTunes purchases; it now works with a host of apps found within the App Store to add an extra layer of security.

⑦ Display

The screen of the iPad is 9.7 inches, while the smaller iPad Mini features a 7.9-inch display. On both screens, the backlit multi-touch display has a special coating to help prevent smearing and smudges from greasy fingerprints.

- **Retina Display:** The newer iPads use more impressive Retina displays to generate sharper video, images and text on pages. The iPad Air 2 is the only tablet in the range to include a fully laminated display and an anti-reflective coating to improve outdoor visibility.

Touchscreen

With no physical keyboard, you control the iPad and enter text by tapping and swiping the display.

REAR

❶ iSight Camera

The initial video camera on the iPad (iPad 1 has no cameras) has been upgraded from a 0.7-megapixel lens that shoots video at 720p to a 5-megapixel lens on later models, which shoots full 1080p HD (high-definition) video.

The range of features includes video stabilization, auto-focus, face detection and geotagging. The iPad Air 2 includes a more impressive 8-megapixel camera and has an additional burst mode, letting you take several images at once.

❷ SIM Card Slot

This holds the micro-SIM card your telecommunications company will give you to access their data networks. The cover is easily removed using the SIM card tool supplied. The latest iPad can connect to the regular 3G or faster 3.5G HSPA+ network and, in countries where they are available, 4G LTE networks.

❶ iSight camera

❻ Side switch

❺ Volume buttons

❷ SIM card slot

❹ Speaker

❸ Dock connector

○ **Apple SIM**: In the iPad Air 2 and iPad Mini 3rd generation Apple has introduced a new kind of SIM card, which will allow you to switch between network operators and data plans without having to physically swap SIM cards. The standard looking nano-SIM card can be found already pre-installed inside the SIM card slot.

> # Hot Tip
>
> **Cleverly, the iPad remembers two volume settings: one for the volume you set when using headphones and the other for the sound level when using the speaker.**

❸ Dock Connector

The original 30-pin dock connector used with iPad 1, 2 and 3 has been changed to the much lighter, smaller Lightning connector on newer models. The dock connector allows you to hook up to your computer, power charger, camera connector and other accessories. As a result of the change many existing accessories will not work with the iPad 4 and newer models.

❹ Speaker

The speaker grill is at the bottom edge of your iPad.

❺ Volume Buttons

With the rocker button, press one end to turn the sound up and the other to turn it down. As you adjust the setting, a box will appear on screen with a speaker icon and a volume strength bar.

❻ Side Switch

This can do one of two things. By default, it is used to lock the orientation of the iPad, so it stays in either vertical (portrait) or horizontal (landscape) mode. If you go to Settings, you can change it to be a mute switch that turns the iPad's volume off.

iPAD BASICS

Getting started with your iPad is simple and opens up a whole new world of entertainment, communication and fun.

SET UP YOUR iPAD

When you get your brand new iPad, there's remarkably little in the box: just the iPad, power cord and not much else. There's no manual, which is one reason why this book can help to get your iPad adventures off to the best start.

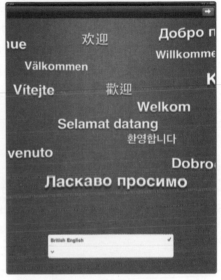

Hot Tip

If you are unsure, during setup, whether you want to activate any services offered, follow the link at the bottom of the screen, which explains more about them.

Step 2: Part of the iPad set up process asks you to select the language you want to use.

Step-by-step

With earlier iPads you had to connect your iPad to your computer – and iTunes – to start the activation process. Since iOS 5.0 you can get going using Wi-Fi.

1. Turn on your iPad by pressing the **Sleep/Wake** button on the top (the Apple logo will appear) and slide the button across to start.

2. Pick the language you want to use, by tapping on it. A blue tick will appear beside it. Tap the **blue arrow** to continue.

3. Choose your location from the list under the map. Usually, your country will show automatically. If not, tap **Show More**, pick your location and tap **Next**.

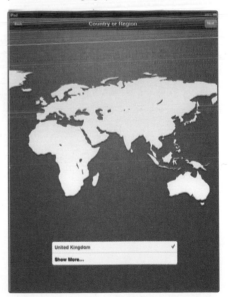

Step 3 (Right): Choose your location by selecting the country you live in from the list under the map.

4. Next, you'll be asked to connect to your Wi-Fi network. A list will open of those available. A lock beside a name shows it is secured and you will need a password to use it. Tap on your chosen network name. Alternatively, you can use your mobile connection.

5. You may want to share your location through mapping and social media apps. To do so, you'll have to turn Location Services on. Tap **Enable Location Services** here and then tap **Next**.

Step 5: Turn on Location Services to share your location through mapping and social media apps.

Hot Tip

Setting up an Apple ID will allow you to get the most out of your iPad. With it, you can download apps, sync your accounts and purchase music, TV shows, films and more.

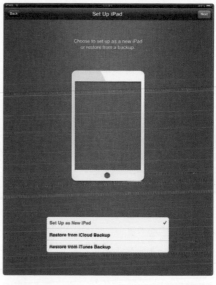

6. The usual terms and conditions appear for you to agree before you can proceed.

7. Now it's time to activate your iPad. If this is your first iPad, select **Set Up as New iPad** and click the **Next** button in the top right hand corner. If you are transferring your data from a previous iPad, select one of the other options to transfer from iCloud or iTunes.

Step 7: Choose whether you want to set up your device as a new iPad or transfer data from an old iPad.

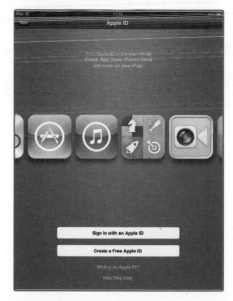

8. To get the most from your iPad, you need an Apple ID, which is also used to set up your iTunes account. Click **Sign In with an Apple ID** if you already have one. Otherwise, **Create a Free Apple ID** takes you through the process.

Step 8 (Right): Set up an Apple ID, or sign in with an existing Apple ID, so that you can download apps from the App Store and access iTunes.

9. Apple then offers to turn on various features. Among them are iCloud, using iCloud for backup, and activating Find My iPad in case you lose your tablet.

10. A list of the phone numbers and email addresses on which you can be contacted via iMessage and FaceTime are shown.

11. You can also set up Siri, Apple's intelligent voice assistant (on iPad 3 and later). Go through a few more screens, including registration of your new iPad, and press the final button to **Start Using iPad**.

Step 9: iCloud is an extremely useful way of storing, backing up and sharing data across different devices.

MOBILE CONNECTIONS

If you have a cellular iPad, you will need to install the SIM card, provided separately by the mobile network company. Simply open the SIM card holder on the side of the iPad – using the pin provided – and put in the SIM card. Turn the iPad on and tap the **Settings** icon, then **Cellular Data** and check this is set to **On**.

Step 10 (Right): Once all the set-up steps are complete, press the Start Using iPad button to begin the fun!

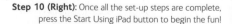

Above: To activate a Wi-Fi connection, choose a network from the list and enter the password.

WI-FI

All models can use Wi-Fi. To connect, tap the **Settings** icon on the Home screen. Tap **Wi-Fi** and then **On**. Under **Choose a Network** you'll see a list of those available. The signal strength is shown by the number of bars on the wireless symbol. The lock shows that it is a secure network and needs a password to access it. Tap the one you want to use to activate it.

CUSTOMIZING YOUR iPAD

Make the iPad your own by modifying the background and changing the ways different apps and controls work.

Step 1: Select Brightness & Wallpaper from the Settings menu to display icons previewing the current wallpaper.

Step 2: Tap the icons to select a new wallpaper image from the pre-supplied options or your own photo albums.

Changing Wallpaper

The wallpaper for your iPad is pasted to your Home screen and on the Lock screen.

1. Tap **Settings** and then **Brightness & Wallpaper**. The large icons under Wallpaper preview the current wallpaper.

2. Tap this and select **Wallpaper** to choose a different, Apple-supplied image, as here, or access one of your own photos.

3. Select the image you want and see it full view. If it's one of your own photos, you can adjust it to fit the screen.

4. Tap **Set Lock Screen** to use it as the wallpaper there or **Set Home Screen** if you want it to be the background for that screen. **Set Both** will use the same image as wallpaper on both screens.

NOTIFICATIONS

While it's good to know what's going on and needs your attention, now you decide when – or if – notifications appear.

Access the Notification Center

- Put your finger on the top of the screen and swipe it down. The **Notification Center** slides into view, showing what requires attention.

- Tap individual items in the **Notification Center** to switch to the app that created them.

- Notifications can also appear on your iPad's Lock screen. Slide your finger on the notification and it will unlock the iPad and go to the relevant app.

- You can select which apps send notifications and the order in which they're displayed by tweaking your settings:

Above: By tapping the Settings icon on the Home screen and selecting Notifications, you can rearrange the order in which you receive notifications and edit which apps you wish to receive them for.

1. Tap the **Settings** icon on the Home screen and select **Notifications**.

2. Tap **Edit** and then use the three-line handles to move the apps up and down to reflect the order you want for the notifications. Select **Done** when you've finished.

3. Tap on the **arrow** beside any of the apps and choose whether you want them in the Notification Center by sliding the button to **On** or **Off**. You can also select the type of **alert** used.

4. For iPads running iOS 8.0, you can also choose whether alerts are shown as a banner at the top of the screen or as an alert that appears in the middle of the Home screen.

INTERACTIVE NOTIFICATIONS

Available on iPads running iOS 8.0, you can now respond to notifications without launching the app. Whether it's a calendar appointment or an iMessage, you can reply from the banner that appears at the top of the screen and from the Lock screen.

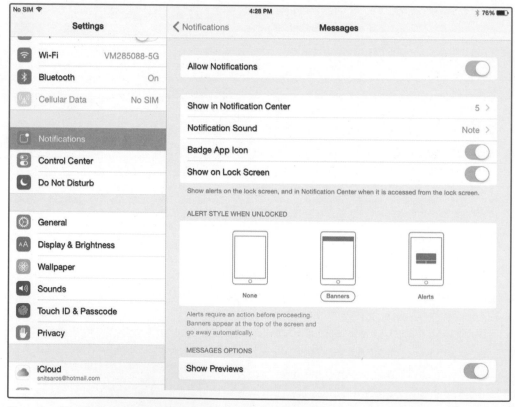

Above: If you have iOS 8, you can now respond to notifications straight from the alert banner or Lock screen.

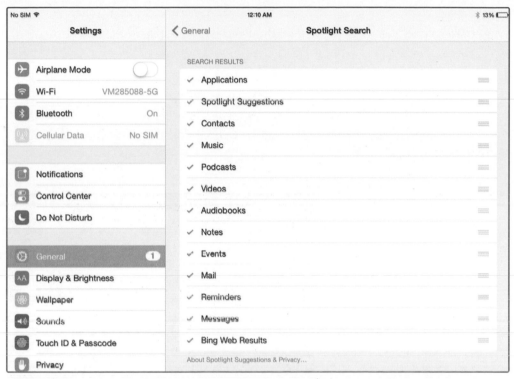

Above: Newer iPad models have the Spotlight search function. To access it, swipe down from the top of the Home screen, type your search term and tap Search.

SEARCH

You know the exact piece of information you need is on your iPad but you can't remember where. **Search** will hunt through all the built-in apps, an individual app or all apps at once. The icon to the left of a Search result shows which app it is from. Simply tap the item to open. The latest iPad models can also use the new Spotlight search to filter through queries on the web, iTunes, the App Store, films and nearby locations.

Hot Tip

The icon to the left of a Search result shows which app it is from. Simply tap the item to open.

PRINT

While the iPad saves paper, there are times when you do need to print something out. Here's the easiest way to do it.

- Built into the iPad is support for printing wirelessly to AirPrint-enabled printers. All that's necessary is for the printer to be on the same wireless network as the iPad. You can print direct to AirPrint-enabled printers from built-in iPad apps such as Mail, Photos, Safari, Notes and Maps.

- To print a document within an app, tap the **arrow icon** then **Print**. Press **Select Printer** and choose one from the list. Set the printer options and tap **Print**.

COMMAND CENTER

Whether you want to skip a track on iTunes or adjust the screen brightness, the Command Center offers shortcuts to key iPad features. To access it, swipe up from the bottom of the Home screen.

Right: Swipe up from the bottom of the Home screen for shortcuts to key iPad features.

iPAD'S OPERATING SYSTEM (iOS)

iOS is Apple's operating system for mobile devices such as the iPad, iPhone, iPod Touch and, just to be different, Apple TV. iOS is regularly updated with new features.

UPDATING WIRELESSLY

Tap **Settings**, **General**, then **Software update**. This shows the version number and if an update is available. If there is a newer version, follow the on-screen instructions to download and install the update. If your battery is less than half-strength, you'll be warned to connect your iPad to a power source.

UPDATING VIA iTUNES

Connect your iPad to your Mac or PC and click on your iPad's name in the top menu bar, then the **Summary** tab. You can see the version and a message stating when iTunes will next automatically check for an update. If you don't want to wait until then, click the **Check for Update** button. If one is available, follow the instructions to download and install.

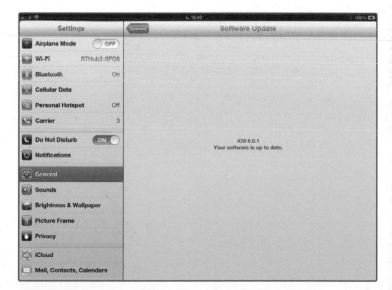

Above: If there is an update available it will be ready for wireless download and installation from the Software Update area.

USING YOUR iPAD

NAVIGATING YOUR iPAD

The iPad is remarkably simple to use, considering the technical complexity behind it. Here's a round-up of the gestures to use to speed your way around your iPad.

Above: Apps such as Contacts and Music display an alphabetic scrollbar on the right-hand side. Simply press the letter you want to go directly to the relevant part of the list.

Tap: The most common gesture, the touch equivalent of the mouse click.

Double-tap: Tap twice in quick succession. Primarily used for zooming in on a web page or section of text.

Tap and hold: Works similarly to the right-click on a mouse. Tap on the screen and hold your finger in place and a small pop-up menu appears. In text, for example, this will give you options for cutting and pasting words or whole sentences.

Scroll: The touch equivalent of using the scroll wheel on a mouse to navigate down a web page quickly. Press your finger lightly on the screen then run it up or down to move through the list or web page.

Flick: An extension of the scroll, this allows you to work your way through a long list, such as Contacts, more quickly. Press your finger gently on the screen then flick up or down. The faster the flick, the quicker the scroll.

Swipe: You can swipe left or right to move through your Home screen pages, your images in Photos or up and down to read text in Safari or Newsstand.

Pinch: To zoom in or to open something, put your index finger and thumb together on the screen and slowly move them apart. To zoom out, do the reverse.

Rotate: Turn everything upside down. Just put two fingers on the screen and make a circular gesture clockwise or anti-clockwise.

Above: You can rotate individual pictures in your photo albums by touching two fingers on the screen and making a circular gesture.

STATUS SYMBOLS

Just like your computer's menu bar, the iPad has a number of status icons at the top of the screen that show what's going on. Icons for your mobile and Wi-Fi connections are on the left, with other services on the right.

Hot Tip

A two-fingered swipe has a different effect in some apps; for example, in Photos it returns you to the thumbnail view of your pictures.

Signal strength: The more bars, the stronger the network signal in your area. One bar shows little to no service, five bars and all is well.

 Carrier: At the end of the signal strength indicator is the name of the mobile data network provider, such as 3 or O2-UK.

 Wi-Fi strength: This radar-like symbol shows if you're connected to a Wi-Fi network. The more visible bars, the stronger the reception.

 Personal hotspot: The two interlinked circles show that your iPad is sharing its high-speed mobile data connection to link a computer or other device, such as an iPod Touch, to the internet. This feature is available only on iPad 3, 4 and Mini.

 Airplane mode: When travelling by air, this switches off any communication systems likely to interfere with the plane's controls and lets you can carry on using other apps.

Hot Tip

Airplane mode turns off GPS, Bluetooth and Wi-Fi, so you won't be able to use any apps, such as Mail and Maps, which rely on these features.

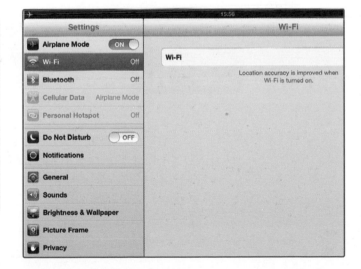

Right: Activate Airplane mode by toggling to On in the Settings menu. Note the plane icon in status bar.

VPN: Shows you are using a Virtual Private Network (VPN) as a secure connection across the internet to your office systems.

Syncing icon: This rotating circle appears when the iPad is trying to make a connection over your Wi-Fi or Bluetooth network.

Battery status: When your battery is charging, this icon shows a small lightning bolt. Beside it the percentage figures show how much battery power is left.

Location services: This arrow appears when an app, such as Maps, is using Location Services.

Play button: This triangular icon appears in the status bar if you're playing a music track in iTunes.

Bluetooth: This is turned on and is being used by your iPad to pair with another device, such as a wireless keyboard.

Above: Set an alarm by scrolling through the numbers wheel until it shows your chosen time.

Alarm clock: Get ready for your early morning wake-up; this shows you have set an alarm in the Clock app.

Do not disturb: The moon icon shows that no notifications will appear on screen and that no sounds will be made while your iPad is locked or sleeping. This feature is not available on iPad 1.

Lock: The small padlock, appearing where the time used to be, indicates that your iPad is locked.

 Orientation lock: If this icon is in the status bar, it means that the orientation has been locked. To unlock it, double-press the Home button, swipe to the right and tap on the orientation button, so the lock disappears.

MULTITASKING

With multitasking you can switch between tasks without having to close them. You can, for example, be using one app – such as your email – and click a link that then opens another, such as Safari, while having other apps from your Calendar to To-Do list open.

Above: Swipe four or five fingers upwards to reveal the Multitasking Bar, which allows you to move quickly between multiple apps and pages.

Multitasking Bar

The Multitasking Bar shows all the apps currently running.

- **To open it**: Double-press on the Home button or use the Swipe Gesture described on page 39 to reveal the Multitasking Bar. The main screen fades away and you'll see the icons of the currently running apps.

- **To switch to another app**: Simply tap the icon for it. The current app swoops away behind the new one, which takes its place full screen.

○ **To shutdown any of the open apps**: Go to the Multitasking Bar and tap-and-hold any icon. This starts jiggling. Tap the red circle with white line – which looks like a No Entry sign – and it is removed from the list.

○ **Swipe**: If you swipe all the way to the right when the Multitasking Bar is open, you have a quick way of accessing key iPad controls. There's the orientation lock (or mute button depending on how the Side Switch is configured), a slider to adjust screen brightness, plus a volume slider and other controls for your music.

Multitasking Gestures

A feature that's unique to the iPad and not available on other iOS devices, such as the iPhone or iPod Touch, is Multitasking Gestures. Using four fingers – and your thumb if you want – you can pinch and swipe to move quickly between different apps and pages.

Hot Tip

To turn Multitasking Gestures on, tap the Settings button on the Home screen and choose General. Scroll down and you'll see the toggle switch to turn the feature on.

○ **Home screen pinch**: Place four or five fingers on screen in any app and bring them together to close it or return to the Home screen.

○ **Swipe to reveal Multitasking Bar**: Open the Multitasking Bar by swiping four or five fingers upwards. To close it again, swipe down.

○ **Swipe to switch apps**: Instead of relying on the Multitasking Bar to move between apps, simply swipe sideways with four or five fingers and you'll go to the next open app.

Above: To access the Multitasking function, turn the feature on in the General area of the Settings app.

USING YOUR iPAD

Once you get used to the touchscreen keyboard, it's quick and easy to use a conventional computer keyboard. In addition, if you decide you don't want to type, ask Siri to do it for you.

ON-SCREEN KEYBOARD

What gives you the power to work on the iPad just as efficiently as any laptop is the virtual keyboard. In apps that use it, simply touch the area of the screen where you want to write and the keyboard appears.

Above: To display numbers and punctuation marks, press the .?123 key on the main keyboard.

Three-in-one Keyboard

The main keyboard just has the letters and basic punctuation, with two shift keys for entering uppercase letters. To type in all caps, double-tap the shift key; tap again to disable. To enter numbers or less frequently used punctuation marks, tap the key marked **.?123** to switch keyboard. To return to the first keyboard, press the ABC key, or to access the third keyboard, which has the least frequently used keys, tap **#+=**.

EDITING TEXT

○ **Magnifier:** It can be fiddly to get the cursor exactly where you want it. To make it easier, tap-and-hold the text until a magnifier appears. Move this around the text and when you find the precise point you want, let go.

○ **To select a word:** Tap the insertion point, and the selection buttons appear. There are options to select that word or all of the document. Double tap a word, and it is selected and highlighted in blue with two grab points at either end. Drag these either way to select more text. You can also move them up or down to select whole paragraphs.

○ **Once the text is selected:** Option buttons appear for cutting or copying it. The Paste option will replace the highlighted text with the last text cut. Depending on the app used, other features, such as styling or text formatting, may be available.

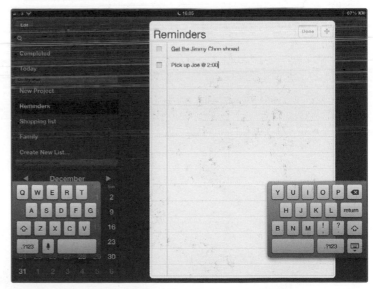

Above: To reveal more of your screen, split the keyboard in two by placing two fingers in the center and sliding them apart.

PREDICTIVE TEXT

Rather like someone watching over your shoulder, the iPad will try to be helpful and guess what you're typing. Its suggestions will appear in a text bubble. Press the spacebar or a punctuation mark to accept it.
If it's wrong, tap the small x in the text bubble.

Hot Tip

You can now say 'Hey Siri' instead of holding down the Home button to activate the iPad's voice assistant. To enable, go to Settings, then General and in the option named Siri, swipe the toggle to Allow Hey Siri.

To stop it, go to **Settings**, **General**, **Keyboard** and turn off **Auto-Correction**. The new QuickType keyboard introduced in iOS 8 can now predict words based on the context of the sentence, and over time learns writing style according to the person you are writing to.

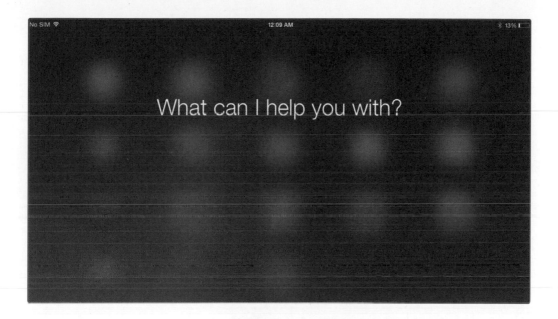

What can I help you with?

VOICE DICTATION

With the arrival of Siri on iPad 3 and later, you can dictate what you want to write, rather than use the on-screen keyboard to type your text.

1. Check that voice dictation is turned on. Press the **Settings** icon, select **General**, followed by **Siri**.

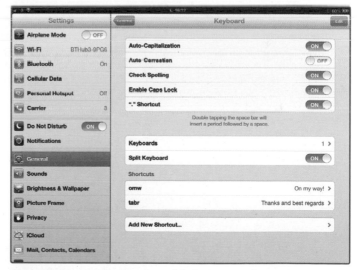

Step 1: Turning on Siri in the General area of the Settings menu allows you to dictate what you want to write.

2. You will need to be connected to the internet, either through Wi-Fi or over the mobile network, as dictation is controlled by Siri. This is the voice-commanded personal assistant in iOS.

3. Open the app you want to use, such as Pages for a document or Mail for email.

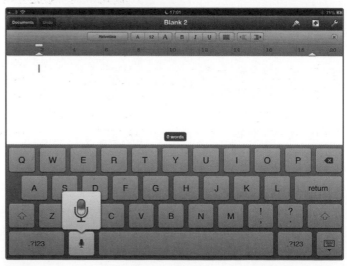

4. Tap the screen, so the on-screen keyboard appears. In the lower left-hand corner is the voice dictation logo, which looks like an old-fashioned radio microphone.

5. Tap this and start speaking. You will need to include punctuation commands, such as comma, new

Step 4: Touch the microphone icon on the on-screen keyboard to begin dictating your text to Siri.

paragraph, etc. Take care to pronounce special symbols, such as the 'at sign' – @ – seen in emails, clearly.

6. When you've finished dictating, tap the microphone icon again. Your text will appear soon.

7. If you make a mistake, or the dictated text is wrongly transcribed, simply tap where you want to edit and the on-screen keyboard appears. Use this to make your corrections. Siri's done well here – only the end of 'fashioned' has been left off.

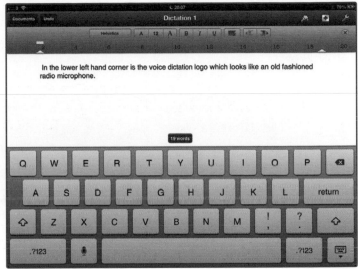

Step 7: You can make corrections using the on-screen keyboard.

FAMILY SHARING

If you are sharing your iPad with the entire family, this new feature added in iOS 8 builds on the Home Sharing feature and now allows you to share purchases made through iTunes, apps and iBooks all without having to use the same Apple ID and without paying extra for every additional download.

> ## Hot Tip
>
> iPads running on iOS 8.0 or above now support third party keyboards like SwiftKey, which can be downloaded from the Apple App Store.

The same credit card needs to be used and can be assigned to up to six Apple device users (including yourself). Other benefits include sharing calendars and the ability to approve purchases made by younger users.

Setting up Family Sharing

1   Go to **Settings** and select **iCloud**. Look for the option entitled **Set up Family Sharing** and press.

2. You'll be prompted to choose the payment method that ties all the purchases together. Click **Continue** when the payment details are correct.

3. There is also the option to share location, to help monitor where other users are. This is optional.

4. When you go back into the Family Sharing option in iCloud, you can now add additional family members. If they are already contacts, email addresses will be pulled through – or you can add them manually.

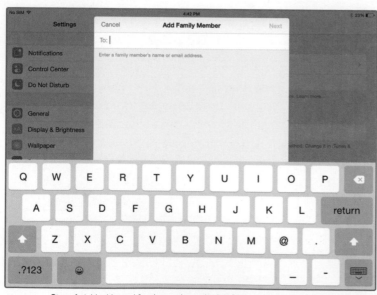

5. You then have the option to choose whether that user requires permission to download apps, which is useful if you plan to let children have access. The permission will pop on your Lock screen to alert you to any purchases.

6. Now pick whether you want to send an invitation to the user or ask the user to add their password.

Step 4: Add additional family members whether from your existing contacts or manually.

CONTINUITY

One of the most innovative features introduced in iOS 8, Continuity brings iPads, iPhones and Mac computers closer together. As long as both are on the same Wi-Fi connection and the Mac runs on the OS X 10 Yosemite operating system, you can start and resume documents, make phone calls and even send and receive text messages on your Mac or vice versa.

There's a series of different useful features that makes up Continuity, and here's our pick of the most useful to use with your iPad.

Setting up Continuity SMS text messages

1. The first thing you need to do is make sure both iPhone and iPad are logged in with the same Apple ID.

2. On your iPhone, go to **Settings** and select **Messages**, Here you'll need to make sure that **Text Message Forwarding** is toggled to **On**.

3. As long as the iPad is on the same Wi-Fi network, you should be able to choose the device you want to forward messages to.

4. A security code should appear on the iPad to ensure it's connecting to the right iPhone.

5. Now you should be ready to make phone calls.

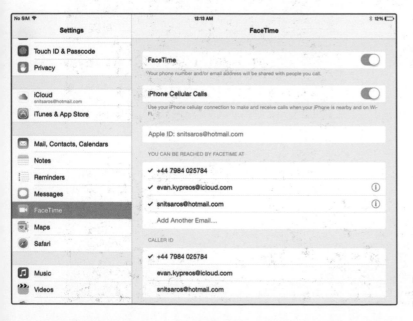

Instant hotspots

If you don't want to pay for a separate data plan for your iPad and your iPhone or you only have a Wi-Fi iPad, this is a way to make getting online on the move much easier.

Left: To receive phone calls on your iPad, select FaceTime in Settings, and switch on iPhone Cellular Calls.

Setting up an instant hotspot

1. Make sure that the iPhone is on a data plan that supports tethering. This means you can share mobile data. You also need to have Bluetooth 4.0 switched on, to run iOS 8.0 or higher and be logged into the same Apple ID account.

2. On the iPhone, turn on the **Personal Hotspot** in the **Settings** menu.

3. On the iPad, go to **Settings**, then **Wi-Fi** and where it reads **Personal Hotspot**, select the iPhone you want to connect to.

> ## Hot Tip
>
> Continuity also allows you to receive calls on your iPad. To set up, go to Settings, FaceTime and turn on iPhone cellular calls.

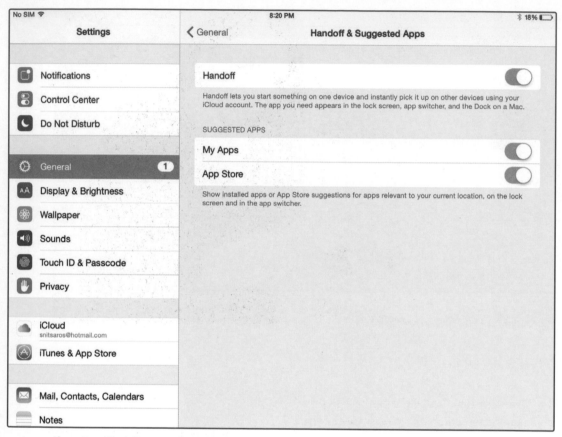

Above: To use Handoff, connect all your devices to the same iCloud account, same Wi-Fi network and switch on Bluetooth.

Handoff

Whether you are working on a document or writing an email, Handoff lets you finish working on another iOS-running device like an iPhone or even a Mac. To activate, all participating devices require Bluetooth 4.0, Wi-Fi support and to be set up on the same Apple ID. The Mac needs to run on OS X 10 Yosemite too. Handoff works with a series of apps like Calendar, Mail, the Safari web browser and Apple's iWork suite.

Setting up Handoff on iPad and Mac

○ On your iPad, go to **Settings** and select **Handoff & Suggested Apps**. Tap the toggle next to Handoff to turn on.

○ On the Mac, go to **System Preferences**, then select **General**. You should see the option to Allow Handoff between this Mac and your iCloud devices. Tick the box to turn on.

GETTING CONNECTED

SURFING THE WEB

Through the built-in Safari browser and your Wi-Fi or mobile connection to the internet, you can surf the web, view your favourite sites, update your blog and download files.

BROWSING

Safari on the iPad is a little different from the one on your Mac or PC. To open it, tap the Safari icon in the dock of commonly used applications at the bottom of the screen.

In the top bar, tap the screen and type the web address – URL – you want to visit, using the on-screen keyboard. As you type, you'll see suggestions of previous pages you've visited, which you can select by tapping the address in the list. Tap **Go** when you've finished.

TAB THAT

Just like your desktop browser, you can have several web pages open at once, in separate tabbed windows. To open a new window, tap the + button at the end of the tab bar and enter the web address. Switch between the windows by tapping the tab you want.

Left: To visit a website, use the on-screen keyboard to type the web address and press Go.

CLOUD BUTTON

If you've been surfing the web using Safari on your Mac, you can carry on from the same place on your iPad by tapping the Cloud icon in the Safari toolbar. This will show you the tabs that are currently open on your other iOS devices and Mac (if it's running the latest operating system), provided they are also set up to use iCloud.

PRIVATE BROWSING

If you don't want to leave a trail of the websites you've visited, you can turn on private browsing. Go to **Settings**, **Safari** and switch on **Private Browsing**. Now Safari won't keep a list of sites you visit, although you also lose the convenience of Safari saving any website login details.

Made a mistake? Clear the address bar at any time by tapping the X button on the far right.

Right: Tap the Cloud icon to access sites, which are currently open on your Mac or other iOS devices, which have iCloud activated.

NAVIGATING THE WEB

Just like your computer browser, Safari lets you move backwards and forwards between open web pages using the left and right pointers on the top bar. However, there are other novel ways to navigate individual pages.

VIEWING WEB PAGES

○ **Scroll the page**: Drag your finger up and down the screen. The scrollbar on the right shows where you are. For faster scrolling, flick your finger up or down the page.

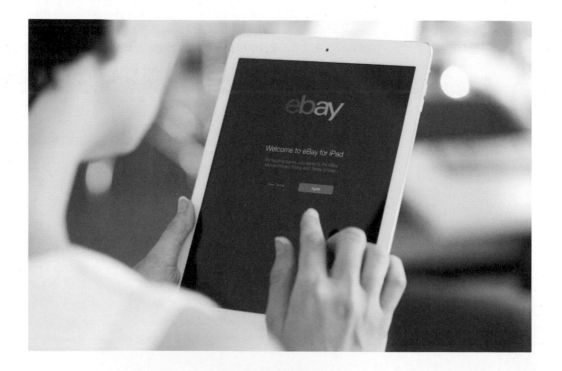

- **Unpinch**: This lets you zoom in on part of the page. Put two fingers together on the screen where you want to enlarge the page and move them apart. Put two fingers either side of the screen and move them together (pinch) to reverse this.

- **Zoom in to images** and text by double-tapping the screen. Zoom out by repeating the double-tap.

- **Once zoomed in**, tap the screen and drag the page left or right. A horizontal scrollbar at the bottom of the screen shows where you are on the page.

Above: You can navigate web pages by pinching and unpinching to zoom in and out, and dragging up and down to scroll.

Hot Tip

If you don't feel like typing your search query, press and hold the Home button until Siri appears. State what you're looking for – e.g. pizza restaurants – and Siri repeats the request and returns the results (iPad 3 or later and iPad Mini or later only).

Above: Press the Home button to search the web by dictating your request to Siri.

SAVE THE WEB

As you browse the web, Safari offers several ways to share the pages you like or save them for viewing later.

SHARING

Tap the **Share** button on the top bar for various ways to spread the word about a web page. Mail the link, text it or post it to your status on Facebook and Twitter.

AIRDROP

You can share content to contacts using iPhones, iPods, iPads and even to Macs. AirDrop uses Wi-Fi and Bluetooth and must be turned on inside the Command Center. Both users must be signed into an iCloud account to be able to send content.

> **Hot Tip**
>
> **Instead of repeatedly filling in your personal contact details on web forms, use AutoFill. Enable it by tapping Settings, Safari and selecting AutoFill preferences.**

READING LIST

If you don't have time to read something that interests you, view it later. Tap the **Share** button, then touch **Add to Reading List**.

To view your Reading List, tap **Bookmarks** and then press the link. Once you have visited the page, it no longer shows in the Unread list but can still be accessed by the All tab.

BOOKMARKS

To add a page to your bookmarks, tap the **Share** button, then **Bookmark**. To access your bookmarks, tap the Open Book icon on the top bar. Using iCloud, you can synchronize your bookmarks between your iPad, computer and other iOS devices, so you always have access to your favourite web pages.

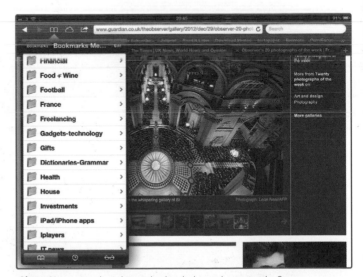

Above: View, visit and reorder your bookmarked pages by tapping the Open Book icon in the top bar.

MESSAGING

Need to send a message to a friend? Using the built-in Messages app, you can text anyone who has an iPhone, iPod Touch or iPad for free – and even send pictures or video.

TEXTING

The beauty of iMessage, the name of Apple's messaging system, is that since iOS 5 it is built in.

How to Text:
Step-by-step

1. Go to **Settings**, **Messages** and make sure that **iMessage** is turned on.

2. Launch the Messages app. If it's not already entered, you'll have to give your Apple ID and password to activate the service. Tap **Sign In**.

3. Enter the email address you want to use to send messages. It can be any you own; it doesn't have to be the same one used with your Apple ID. Tap **Next**.

4. Open **Messages** and tap the **New Message** icon (Pen and Paper) at the top of the screen. Start writing in the **To:** line and a pop-up box listing your relevant contacts will appear. You can send a message to any name that has a blue speech bubble beside it.

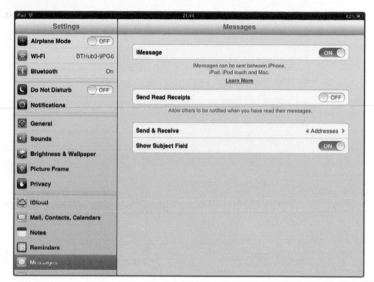

Step 1: Check iMessage is turned on by selecting the Messages option within Settings.

Step 4: Tap the New Message icon, start typing in the To: box to bring up other iMessage users.

5. Tap the name of the selected iMessage user, type your message and press the blue **Send** button.

6. In true messaging style, your conversation is shown as a series of speech bubbles: your message on the right, your friend's reply on the left. When someone is replying to you, there's a bubble with three dots in the chat window.

Step 5: After selecting the recipient, type your message and press the Send button.

GROUP MESSAGING

You can send messages to a group. For example, to let everyone know what the arrangements are for an evening out, just write their names in the **To:** line or select them from your Contacts using the + button.

Step 6: Sent and received messages are shown in speech bubbles.

Hot Tip

Message threads can now be customized, letting you name specific threads, add or remove users and create a Do Not Disturb mode so, for example, you don't get interrupted by a group conversation when you are in a meeting.

GO MULTIMEDIA

To add a picture, tap the Camera icon beside the text box. In the pop-up box, choose to send an existing image from your photo library or select **Take Photo or Video** and add a new picture or video clip.

EMAIL

The Mail app lets you connect to your online email account and will even notify you when you've got mail. It's a great way to keep up with your emails and stay in touch.

SETTING UP ACCOUNTS

To access your email, you first need to set up details of your email service. With some of the main email programs, such as Microsoft Outlook or Apple Mail, you can transfer these settings using iTunes. Otherwise you can do it directly on your iPad.

Transfer Your Email Settings

1. First, connect your iPad with your computer, using a USB cable or wirelessly over your Wi-Fi network.

2. Open iTunes on your computer and you'll see your iPad listed on the top bar.

3. Click on the **Info** tab and go to **Sync Mail Accounts**. Select the accounts you want on your iPad and click **Apply** or **Sync**. Only your account settings – none of your emails – are copied across.

> ## Hot Tip
>
> Tap and hold the Home button, ask Siri to 'Check my email', and a list of the latest emails appears. Tap the one you want, and it opens in the main Mail window (iPad 3 or later and iPad Mini models only).

Add Email Accounts Direct to Your iPad

Although you access your emails through the Mail app, you set up the account using the main Settings app.

1. Tap **Settings**, then **Mail**, **Contacts**, **Calendars** and **Add Account**.

Step 2: Choose your email provider from the list, or tap Other to add your account details.

2. You will see several of the most popular web-based mail services listed. There's also Microsoft Exchange, which is used by many schools and companies for their email servers.

3. Tap the button for your email service if it's listed and enter your name, email address, password and a description, then tap **Save**.

4. If it's not listed, select **Other** and enter your account details manually – you can get them from your Internet Service Provider.

RECEIVE MAIL

1. When you tap the Inbox, there's a list of all your emails. Each one shows the sender's name, when it was sent, the subject line and a preview of the first few lines of the message.

2. Drag the list down to check for new messages. Tap the Message preview, and the full message opens in the main window.

Above: To find particular emails stored in your mail box, type a phrase in the Search box and select the relevant option to choose where to search.

3. If you tap the sender's name, you have the option to add them as a new contact or add the email address to an existing contact.

4. Flick to scroll through the message, or messages if it's a thread. Double-tap or pinch to zoom in on the text or images. Touch and hold an image for options to save, copy or share it.

5. If there's a word in the message you're not familiar with, look it up. Double-tap to select the word, using the grab handles if necessary, and then tap **Define** in the pop-up menu bar.

6. To zip back to the start of the email, tap the iPad status bar at the top of the screen.

Hot Tip

iOS 8 allows you to view other emails while you are composing a new one simply by swiping down.

SEARCH MESSAGES

This is handy if you want to find that elusive email. Tap in the **Search** box and enter your phrase. Then tap the relevant button for where to search – the **From** or **To** fields, the **Subject** line or the new **All** option, which searches the body of the message as well. From the results, select the emails you want and click the **Edit** button to delete/archive, move or mark them, as appropriate.

DELETE MESSAGES

To delete a message, flick its title in the message list. If the email is open, you can also use the **Delete** button in the top bar. To delete several emails at once, click the **Edit** button, select the messages and click the red **Delete** button.

SEND EMAIL: STEP-BY-STEP

1. To write a new email, tap the Pen and Paper icon at the top of Mail; or if you're replying or forwarding a message, select the curved arrow at the top.

2. In the **New Message** box that opens, add the recipient's email address. You can type this in or tap the **+** sign to select them from your Contacts list.

3. If you choose the wrong name, simply tap it and press the backspace key on the keyboard to delete it.

4. Add anyone you're copying the message to. Use Bcc – blind copying – if you're sending it to lots of people, such as a mailing list, and you don't want to show all their addresses.

5. Tap **From** and choose the account you want to use to send it. Add your Subject line and start typing your message.

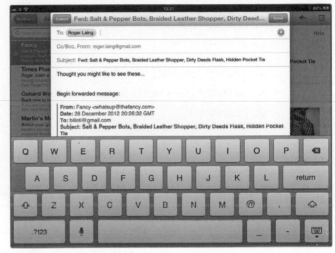

Above: Forward a message by clicking on the curved arrow at the top of an email and select the Forward option.

6. To format the text, tap and use the grab handles to select all the text you want to include. Tap **BIU** and then choose **Bold**, **Italic** or **Underline**. From this menu you can also choose **Quote Level** to increase or decrease the indentation on any text quoted from the original message.

7. To add an attachment, tap where you want to add it and select **Insert Photo or Video** from the pop-up menu. Select the photo source, then the photo and tap the **Use** button.

8. When you're happy with your message, press the **Send** button in the top-right corner. If you're not yet ready to send, tap the **Cancel** button and choose the **Save Draft** option.

Hot Tip

If you forward an email, you can include attachments from the original, which you can't if you just Reply to a message.

VIDEO CALLING

If you have an iPad 2 or later, you can use the built-in cameras to have great video chats with other Apple users via FaceTime to reach more of your contacts.

FACETIME

With the iPad's FaceTime app you can make free video calls over the internet anywhere in the world.

Setting up Your Video Calls

As well as a camera-equipped iPad, you'll need to be connected to the internet to use FaceTime. The person you are calling must also have an iPad, iPhone or iPod Touch with forward-facing camera, or a Mac computer with camera, and FaceTime.

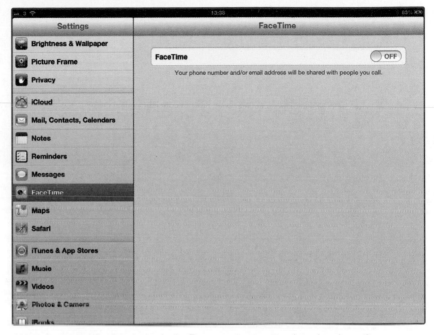

Above: Activate FaceTime by selecting the FaceTime option in your settings list and toggling to On.

1. Activate FaceTime by going to **Settings**, then **FaceTime**.

2. FaceTime identifies you through your Apple ID, the email address and password you use for accessing the App Store. You can either use your existing ID or create a new one.

3. Next select which of your email addresses to use as your contact point with your FaceTime account.

4. You can use your mobile connection for video chat. However, depending on your price plan, a FaceTime chat could use up much of your monthly data allowance, and with 3G connections the quality may be poor.

FaceTime Calls: Step-by-Step

1. To make a FaceTime call, tap the **FaceTime app** to open it. A list of your contacts is on the right. If the person you want isn't listed, tap the + icon, add their details and tap **Done**.

2. To make a call, tap the name of the person, then their FaceTime phone number or email address.

Step 3: Video images of yourself and your contact appear once the call is set up.

3. When they answer, there will be a pause while the video chat is set up. Once connected, your face will shrink to a small thumbnail, while the person you are calling is pictured in the main window.

4. During the call, drag your picture to a different position if it's in the way.

Step 5: Tap the Microphone icon to mute the sound, and tap again to unmute.

5. Tap the Microphone icon on the menu to temporarily mute the sound (the picture won't be affected). Tap again to restore it.

6. Tap the Camera icon to switch from the front camera, showing you, to the back camera, which will show what's around you.

7. To finish the chat, tap the Telephone icon marked **End**.

Step 6: Tap the Camera icon to change between using your front and back iPad cameras.

LOCATION SERVICES

Location Services combine information from the iPad's built-in compass with Wi-Fi, mobile and GPS data to locate where you are.

EXPLORE WITH MAPS

The iPad now has its own Maps app, which enables you to go local – and find the nearest French restaurant or cinema complex – or international. It provides step by step directions and also shows traffic conditions.

Getting Started with Maps

An internet connection – either Wi-Fi or mobile – is needed for Maps to draw down the mapping information. It also relies on Location Services for many of its features. Make sure these are on by going to **Settings**, **Privacy**, and turning on **Location Services**.

Find a Location

> ### Hot Tip
>
> On iPads with Cellular (3G and 4G), the built-in GPS will be used to determine your location more accurately, which can run down your battery faster.

1. Tap the Maps app, then type the name of the place you're looking for in the Search bar. You can search by geographic features, place names, neighbourhood names, street addresses, landmarks, business names and so on.

2. If you're looking for somewhere nearby, such as a coffee shop or theatre, tap the compass arrow to zoom in on your current location.

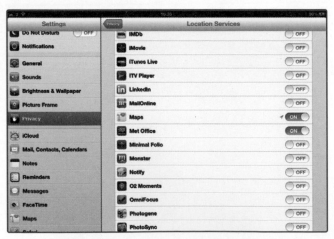

Above: Activate Maps by making sure it is toggled to On in the Settings menu.

3. Maps drops several pushpins on the map with a black bar over the best match. Tap the **i** icon to open the Info window.

4. This tells you more about the location and may include photos, reviews, directions to and from the location, or a link to the website. It also has options to add it to Contacts, share the location on Facebook and Twitter or bookmark it.

Get Directions

To get directions to a location, by car, on foot or using public transport, tap the **Directions** button. Enter where you are and where you're going in the **Start** and **End** fields. Maps displays the route – and any alternatives – along with time and distance information.

Step-by-step Navigation

With the help of Siri, Maps offers step-by-step GPS navigation, similar to the sat-nav in a car or handheld system. It will also store maps of a very large surrounding area so you can still browse and use GPS navigation when you don't have Wi-Fi or mobile data coverage.

Above: Tap the i icon to open the Info window to find out more information about the location the pin is marking, including photos, reviews and directions. You can also share the location with others.

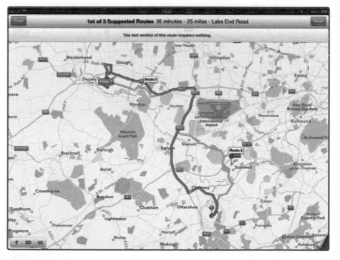

Above: Maps will display alternative routes to your destination, with times and distances noted.

Hot Tip

Let Siri be your travelling companion. Siri can find locations, tell you what points of interest or services are nearby and get directions for your trip (iPad 3 or later).

Twitter

Facebook

Pinterest

Tumblr

Skype

YouTube

Vimeo

Badoo

VK

SoundCloud

Google

Flipboard

Messages

Mail

APPS

GET AND USE APPS

Your iPad comes with a host of apps already loaded, covering the basics from writing notes to playing music. When you want to do more, such as tracking the stars or mind mapping, you can be sure there's an app for it.

FINDING NEW APPS

There's no shortage of apps for your iPad. Currently, there are more than 500,000 free or paid-for apps in the App Store that are specifically designed for the iPad.

You get new apps through Apple's App Store, which is accessed through iTunes on your computer or the App Store app, pre-loaded on the iPad.

Apple ID

To use the App Store, you have to be connected to the internet (via Wi-Fi or mobile) and have an Apple ID. You probably entered this when you activated your iPad. If not, go to **Settings**, **iTunes & App Stores** (**Store** on iPad 1) and enter your details or create a new ID.

Using the App Store App

Accessing the App Store from the iPad itself lets you download new apps directly. Tap the App Store icon to open it and you'll see there are five buttons on the lower toolbar.

- **Featured**: Good for browsing, this screen shows new and noteworthy apps, what's hot and so on. Along the top you can select apps from specific categories, such as games or education.

Above: When the App Store is open, five useful buttons are displayed on the lower toolbar.

Above: Choosing the iPad link in iTunes on your computer allows you to download apps and then sync them to your iPad.

○ **Top Charts**: Shows the most popular paid-for and free apps, as well as the top-grossing apps in the store. Scroll down to see more.

○ **Explore**: Here Apple will recommend apps to download. Enable location sharing to find out popular apps downloaded in your current location.

○ **Purchased**: This lists all the apps (both paid-for and free) you have downloaded to any device, such as your computer, using the same Apple ID. If you've deleted an app you want to restore, find it in the list and tap the Cloud icon to download it. You won't have to pay again.

○ **Updates**: The badge shows how many updates are available for the apps on your iPad. Click the **Update** or **Update All** button to download and install them.

Step 1: Clicking the i in the bottom-right corner of an app icon, or tapping the icon itself, opens a pop-up information window.

iTunes

Open iTunes on your computer and click **iTunes Store** on the top bar, then **App Store** from the top menu. Click the iPad button at the top of the screen to select that section of the store.

CHOOSING YOUR APPS

To find out more about an app, click its icon to access a dedicated page with details of what it does, screenshots, customer ratings and reviews.

Hot Tip

In the purchased section, tap Not on This iPad and you'll see all the apps you have bought that have not yet been downloaded to your iPad.

Step 2: The pop-up information window allows you to read ratings and reviews before you decide to download an app.

Step-by-step

1. Once you've found the app you want, tap the icon for the app and the info screen opens.

2. Scroll down to read a description of the app or use the tabs to see ratings and reviews by other customers or related apps from the same developer.

3. Tap the price button and then tap **Buy**. If it's not a paid-for app, tap the **Get** button, then **Install App**.

4. To stop you buying the same app twice, the button now says **Open**, **Install** or **Update** if you have previously downloaded the app.

Step 3: Once you have decided to download an app, tap the Buy or Free button and then Install App button.

5. You may be asked to enter your Apple ID and password. Tap **OK** when ready.

6. The app's dimmed icon appears on your iPad with a blue progress bar at the bottom. You can move off the page and open other apps while this is happening. Once the download is complete, the app appears on your Home screen, with a **New** flash across the corner, and is ready to open.

Above: New apps will appear in your homescreen with a 'New' banner across the corner, which remains until the app is opened.

7. If the download is interrupted for any reason, it will re-start automatically the next time you connect to the internet.

iTUNES DESKTOP APP

Buying an app in iTunes from your computer works in the same way as on the iPad. Select the app and click the price button. This time, though, it is downloaded to your computer.

USING APPS

Now you've downloaded your apps, how do you go about using them?

Hot Tip

Tap an app to pause download (useful if there are other apps you want to get first). Tap again to restart.

Open and Close Apps

Simply tap the app's icon to open it. To close it and return to the Home screen, just press the Home button. To fully close it, double-press the Home button to open the Multitasking Bar. Press the app's icon and when it starts jiggling, tap the red circle in the corner.

Remove Apps

To delete an app, tap and hold its icon, then press the small white **X** in a white circle that appears in the top-left corner.

Above: Delete an app by tapping and holding an icon until it starts jiggling, and then pressing the X.

Changing App Settings

Most apps keep the options for changing the way they work inside the app itself. Confusingly, though, some apps have a second set of options inside the iPad's Settings app. To access these, tap the Settings icon and select the app from the list on the left. The available options are shown on the right.

Hot Tip

If you tap and hold an app and the small black X doesn't appear, it means it is one of the default apps, pre-loaded on the iPad. These can't be deleted.

SYNCING

It's easier than ever to keep your personal information, music, video files and apps on your iPad in sync using iTunes, iCloud or other online cloud services.

SYNCING WITH iTUNES

As well as keeping all your information up-to-date, syncing is a good safety measure. Each time you sync your iPad with iTunes, a backup is made of all your information. If you lose your iPad or it needs to be reset, you can restore all your data from these backups. It is also the quickest way to transfer large files, such as photos, music or videos.

Syncing by USB: Step-by-step

1. Connect your iPad to the computer by USB cable. Open iTunes on your computer, and your iPad is listed in the top bar.

2. Click the **Summary** tab and you'll see information about your iPad, along with various options.

> **Hot Tip**
>
> Sync all your apps to your iPad automatically, no matter where they were originally downloaded. Tap the Settings icon then iTunes & App Stores (Store on iPad 1) and go to the Automatic Downloads section. Slide the switch beside Apps to On.

3. Select the **Info** tab for options to sync your contacts, calendars and email accounts with related Apple apps on the iPad.

Step 1: To sync your iPad with your computer connect via USB cable. You can then click the Summary tab and select options to sync contacts, calendars and email accounts.

4. Select the **Music** tab and check **Sync Music**.

5. Go through the other tabs – Apps, Tones, Movies, TVShows, Podcasts, Books and Photos – and select what you want to sync. If some of the tabs mentioned aren't visible, don't worry: it just means you have none of that type of content in your iTunes library.

6. When finished, click **Apply** to start the sync.

Syncing Wirelessly

Instead of connecting by USB cable to sync, you can use Wi-Fi. To do so, you first have to connect your iPad with iTunes using a USB cable.

1. Your iPad will show in the top bar in iTunes. Click this and scroll to **Options** on the **Summary** tab.

2. Check the box next to **Sync with this iPad over Wi-Fi** and click **Apply** in the bottom-right corner.

Above: Set up wireless sync using iTunes so that you can sync your devices over Wi-Fi.

3. To sync wirelessly, your iPad has to be connected to a power source and be on the same Wi-Fi network as the computer. The computer must also have iTunes open. If you still don't see your iPad in the list of devices, quit and restart iTunes or restart your iPad.

4. Configure your sync options just as you would with the USB connection.

Hot Tip

If you check Manually Manage Music and Videos, automatic syncing is turned off. To move songs and movies, first go to the View menu in iTunes and select Show Sidebar. Then drag and drop tracks or clips from your iTunes library on to the iPad icon.

iCLOUD

Apple's online service enables you to keep everything in sync and store your music, photos, documents and apps securely. It also brings access to iCloud Drive where you can edit documents, and changes will appear in the original location.

Step-by-step

1. **To set up and configure iCloud**: tap **Settings**, then select **iCloud**. Sign in with your Apple ID and password, or create one if you haven't yet done so.

2. **Choose which iCloud services you want to use**: slide the switch to On.

3. **Mail, Contacts, Calendars, Reminders and Notes**: these sync with the relevant apps on the iPad.

4. **Safari**: This syncs your bookmarks, any open tabs and reading list (that is, web pages you've saved to read later).

5. **Photo Stream**: When you take a photo with any iOS device you have, it will be shared and show up in the Photo Stream of the iPad.

Step 2 (Left): To choose which iCloud services you want to use, toggle switches to On or Off accordingly.

6. Documents & Data: Currently works with Apple's office documents, Pages, Numbers and Keynote, but third-party developers can make their apps use it as well.

7. Find My iPad: Help to locate your lost or stolen iPad.

8. Storage & Backup: Sends your data wirelessly to iCloud.

ENTERTAINMENT

YOUR PHOTOS

The iPad is the complete photographer's kit – able to capture great photos, display them in their full beauty on a high-definition screen and store thousands of pictures in your own electronic album.

TAKING A PHOTO

1. To take a photo, tap the Camera app.

2. To switch to the rear camera, tap the camera icon with the curved arrows either side.

3. You'll see a square white box appear on the screen. This is the focus box. Tap anywhere on the image and the camera centres on that part of the picture.

4. When using the rear camera, tap the image with two fingers together and push them apart to zoom in on the area you want to shoot.

5. When ready, take your shot by pressing the round camera icon on the screen.

6. The pictures you've taken can be viewed in the Camera Roll, the small square box in the bottom-left corner. Tap the image to bring up the controls, which are the same as those in the Photos app.

Step 3: Tap anywhere on screen to focus on that part of the picture, as indicated by a white frame.

EDIT YOUR PHOTOS

However good or bad a photographer you are, the iPad's image-editing tools can make your pictures look better.

Photos App

The Photos app (for iPad 2 and later) gives you the basic tools to make your pictures better.

Hot Tip

If you change your mind about the last edit, tap the Undo button. If you want to undo all of the changes you've applied, tap the Revert to Original button.

- **To start editing**: tap the Photos app with its easily recognizable colourful flower-shaped icon.

- **To edit**: Select the photo you want to enhance and tap the **Edit** button.

- **Editing tools**: Buttons for the four main editing tools appear along the bottom of the screen:

1. **Rotate**: This lets you alter the angle of the picture to straighten the image.

2. **Enhance**: Use the Magic wand icon to adjust the colour and contrast of your images automatically.

Above: Use the Photos app to edit your photos by rotating, enhancing, removing red-eye, cropping and constraining proportions.

3. **Red-eye**: Photos removes this by re-colouring the eye. Tap the Red-Eye button and then on the mis-coloured eye. Tap on each eye affected, then press **Apply** to save your changes.

4. **Crop**: Resize your pictures by tapping the Crop button and then pushing the corners of the grid that appears to adjust the frame.

5. **Constrain**: If you're planning to print your photos, you can constrain the crop ratios to match. Simply press the Constrain button at the bottom and select the proportions you want.

Above: Delete groups of photos by selecting the Edit button and then tapping photos to delete; they will be marked with a blue tick. Once you have finished selecting, tap the Delete button.

DELETING PHOTOS

To delete a single photo, tap the photo you want to delete, then the Dustbin icon and press the red **Delete Photo** button. To delete a group of photos, tap the **Edit** button followed by each photo you want to delete.

SCREENSHOTS

Want to capture an image of what's on your iPad screen? Press the Sleep/Wake button at the top of the iPad and the Home button at the same time, then release. There'll be a flash of white light, a camera click and the image will appear in your Camera Roll.

SHARING PHOTOS

The iPad is a great digital hub for collecting, managing and adding special effects to your photos before sharing them online.

iCloud Photo Stream

Copy your photos to Apple's online storage service, iCloud, and they can be automatically pushed out and received wirelessly on your computer (Mac and PC) or iOS devices.

Sharing Your Photo Stream

Share individual pictures from your Photo Stream with friends and family you choose.

1. First, tap **Settings**, **iCloud**, **Photo Stream** and turn on **Shared Photo Streams**.

2. Open the Photos app, tap **Photo Stream**, then the **Edit** button. Select the photo(s) you want to show off to others and tap the **Share** button in the top-left corner.

3. In the pop-up window write the email address of the person you're sharing it with, or tap the + sign with the blue background to select from your Contacts list.

4. Give it a name and select whether you want anyone to be able to browse this shared Photo Stream via iCloud.com, then tap **Next**. Add a comment if desired and click **Done**.

Hot Tip

iCloud provides unlimited free storage for music and apps, etc. that you buy through iTunes, as well as for your Photo Stream. However, there's only 5GB of free storage for your documents, mail, other photos and backups, although you can purchase more space as needed.

5. If your contacts use iOS 6 or later, they can see the shared Photo Stream in the Photos app, or iPhoto app on the Mac if it runs the latest operating system.

6. If not, it's still possible for them to view the photo albums directly on iCloud.com, but they will need an Apple ID.

YOUR VIDEOS

Shooting and editing video is so easy on the iPad that you will soon be creating movie clips to share on the internet. Go viral, and your clip could be the latest online sensation.

VIDEO RECORDING

Point and tap is all you need to do to start recording your video, provided you've got an iPad 2 or later.

Shooting Video

The video recorder is built in to the Camera app you use to take photos.

1. To start, simply tap the Camera app and slide the switch in the bottom-right corner to video.

2. Point the camera at the scene you want to capture and tap the recording button in the centre-right of the screen.

3. A bell sound marks the start of recording and the red dot in the middle of the camera icon starts flashing. A timer showing how long you've been recording appears in the top-right corner.

4. To finish recording, tap the record button again.

Step 2: Start recording your video by tapping the red recording button to the centre-right of the screen.

EDITING VIDEO

Tidy up your video by using the Camera app to trim unwanted footage from the beginning and end of your clip.

Simple Editing

1. Once you've shot your video, tap the Camera Roll in the bottom-left corner to view the clip.

2. If the top bar is not visible, tap the screen so it appears. In the middle is a timeline of your video, with the cursor showing where you are in the clip.

3. Around the timeline is a grey border with a handle at either end. Press one of these, and the border will turn yellow.

4. Drag the left handle to the right to trim the start of the video, or the right handle to the left to alter the end.

Step 2: Tap the screen to show a timeline of your video, with the cursor marking where you are in the clip.

5. Hold your finger down on one of the handles to zoom in and place your end point more precisely.

6. Tap the **Trim** button. Select **Trim Original**, and the existing video clip is replaced by the trimmed version. Tap **Save as New Clip** to keep both versions.

Step 6: Tap the Trim button and then choose between Trim Original and Save as New Clip.

SHARE YOUR VIDEOS

Once you have the perfect movie, the iPad makes it simple to share your video with friends, family or the wider world of the Internet, via YouTube and Facebook. Tap the **Share** button in the Camera Roll and select your preferred option.

Hot Tip

It's best to have your iPad in horizontal view when running iMovie as you can see more of your timeline and the editing controls.

ENTERTAINMENT CENTER

The iPad is as good a music player as any, with the advantage of a bigger screen to browse through your collection.

USING THE MUSIC APP

This is the place to play all your audio content, whether it's music and audiobooks from iTunes, taken from your CDs or downloaded from the internet.

Play Music

By default, Music is one of
the main buttons in the
Dock that's accessible at
the bottom of every
Home screen.

1. Tap the Music icon to
    open it, then **Songs** and
    the name of the song
    you want to play.

2. In the music controls at
    the top of the screen,
    press the **Play** button (a
    right-pointing triangle)

Above: The Music app appears by default as one of the apps in the Dock at the bottom of the Home screen.

    to start the song. While the song is playing, this changes to the Pause button
    (marked by two vertical lines). Press this at any time to pause the music and press
    again to restart.

3. In the center section the
    red line (playhead)
    moves to the right along
    the scrubber bar to show
    how far you are through
    the song. Tap and move
    the playhead backward
    and forward, and you can
    move to a different part
    of the song.

Hot Tip

To listen to your music, you can play it
through the built-in speaker, attach headphones
through the headphone jack, use wireless
stereo headphones paired with your iPad
via Bluetooth or play through your TV
using AirPlay.

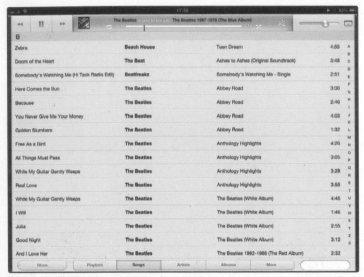

Above: The iPad music player displays the controls, scrubber bar and volume slider at the top.

Above: Tap a thumbnail to display your music in album view, swipe through the album covers to start playing songs automatically.

4. You'll also see time counters at either side. On the left it shows how long the song has been playing. On the right it shows how much time remains before the song ends.

5. Above the progress bar you'll see the name of the song that's playing and the artist. To the left, tap the **Repeat** button (two arrows in a loop) to repeat all the songs in that playlist. Tap it twice to play the current song again. To the right, tap the **Shuffle** button (two arrowed lines meeting and separating) and the songs in the playlist will be played in a random order.

6. On the far left, tap the **Back** button to go to the previous song or the **Forward** button to move to the next song. If the song is playing, tapping the Back button just returns to the start of the track.

ADDING MUSIC

You can add music directly to your iPad through the iTunes app or sync music gathered from other sources (as long as it isn't copy protected), through your computer.

Using the iTunes App

Access the online music store to download music directly to your iPad.

1. Tap the app to go online to the iTunes store and select **Music** at the bottom.

Step 1: Once the app is launched, select Music and browse or search to find the song or album you want.

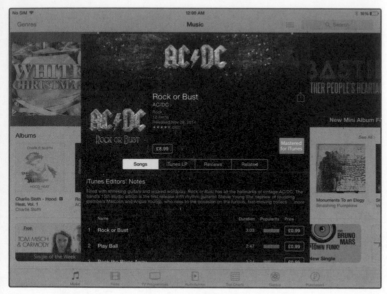

Step 6: Tap the price button to the right of the track to purchase it.

2. If there's a particular genre you like, select it using the buttons at the top of the screen. If the genre you want isn't visible, tap **More** to see others.

3. Scroll down the page and you can see different selections. If you know what you want, use the **Search** box at the top.

4. Once you have selected an album or song, tap to go through to the information page. This includes details of the artist, the release date and average rating by other iTunes users, plus the price button. Underneath is a listing of the track(s).

5. Tap the song title to listen to a 90-second sample of the track.

6. To buy an individual track, tap the price button to the right and then the Buy button. If it's the album on which the track features that you want to buy, tap the price button at the top of the page.

STREAMING MUSIC

Instead of storing and playing your own music, you can get songs, radio shows, concerts and more streamed, on demand, to your iPad.

Airplay

For great sounds around the home, you can use AirPlay to play music from your iPad through AirPlay-enabled speakers. As well as the music, all the information about it, such as the song title, artist's name, playing time and so on, are also streamed across your WI-FI network.

Using AirPlay

1. To use AirPlay, tap your Music app to open. In the top-right corner you'll see the AirPlay symbol. Tap this to open the options box. You'll see the iPad and any other AirPlay-capable devices, such as Apple TV, on your home network.

2. Select the receiver you want to use and a tick appears beside it. In Music, tap a song and it will start to play through the device you selected.

3. Control the sound from your iPad, using Music's audio controls.

4. To return playback to the iPad, tap the AirPlay icon again and select iPad from the list.

Right: Use AirPlay to play music from your iPad through AirPlay capable devices with Hi-Fi speakers, such as Apple TV.

GAMES

When it comes to gameplay, the iPad's large screen gives it a natural advantage over its smaller screen rivals, particularly if you have a Retina display to display the even higher quality graphics.

GAMES STORE

Download games direct to the iPad from the App Store. Simply tap the App Store icon to open and select **Games** from the top bar. In the box that opens you can select All Games categories or choose the one that interests you most.

Hot Tip

Playing with touchscreen controls takes a little getting used to compared with physical controllers, so it might be as well to practise before challenging friends.

Above: See which games in the App Store are most popular by clicking on Top Charts.

Popular Games

There are thousands of games available in the App Store, so it's good to get personal recommendations. To see what others are playing, select the App Store, tap the **Games** button on the top menu and then **Top Charts** at the bottom.

Here you can see the most popular free and paid-for games, as well as those that have grossed the most money.

WORKING

DOCUMENTS

While a touchscreen keyboard may not be as practical as the one on your computer for creating long or complex documents, it is still possible to produce some great-looking work.

WRITING ON YOUR iPAD

Given that it is a mobile app, Pages is a powerful word processor. It is a paid-for app, so you will have to buy and download the program from the App Store, unless it came free with your iPad.

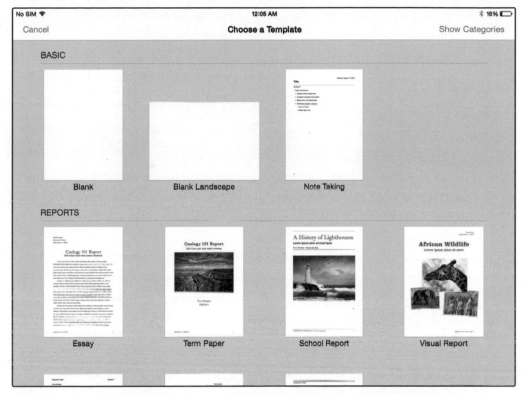

Above: Pages allows you to choose a template from existing formats, or create your own by selecting the Blank option.

Creating a Document

1. Tap **Pages** to open it. The first time it's launched, the Welcome screen offers different options, such as using iCloud to store Pages documents.

2. On the Documents screen, tap the + button in the top-left corner.

Hot Tip

Although there is no PC version of the iWork suite, the files can be saved and transferred in a format that can be used by Office-compatible programs or viewed as PDFs.

3. Choose a Template from the selection, which includes pre-formatted documents, such as different letter and report styles. To create your own, select **Blank**.

4. When you open a template, it will include dummy text. To edit this and replace it with your own, double-tap the screen, and the keyboard will appear.

WORKING WITH iWORK

Pages is part of the iWork suite of programs, which also includes Numbers for spreadsheets and Keynote for presentations. The iPad apps don't have all the features of the Mac versions of the programs, but they are now all free when you buy a new iPad.

If you have iCloud set up on your iPad, the three iWork apps will automatically back up their documents to Apple's servers. The changes are then synced to your Mac and iDevices, so any alterations made to your documents on the go are immediately available when you're back in the office.

Sharing iWork Files

While iCloud makes it simple to move your iWork documents between your Mac or PC and different iDevices, there are other ways to share your files.

Right: Share your documents by selecting from the options in the Share and Print menu.

Sharing Documents

When the document is open in Pages, Numbers or Keynote, tap the Tools button – with the Spanner icon – at the top, then select **Share and Print**. You'll have the option to attach to an email, print, open in another app, copy to iTunes or transfer to a network server via the web.

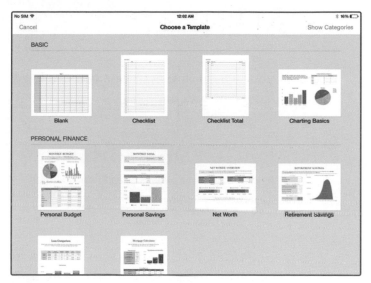

Above: Numbers offers a range of template options.

Dealing with Numbers

Numbers for iPad lets you create and edit your spreadsheets on the go. Even if you have a spreadsheet that wasn't created with Numbers, you can work on it, as the program can open Excel documents or spreadsheets saved as comma-separated value (.csv) files.

Creating Presentations

If a presentation is needed quickly or there are some last minute changes to your slides, Keynote on the iPad is the answer.

Right: When using Keynote for presentations you can change styles by tapping the Paintbrush icon and selecting from the options displayed.

CALENDAR

With your iPad digital assistant you can keep up-to-date with all your calendars – at work and play.

MANAGE YOUR SCHEDULE

The Calendar is a core app that's already on your iPad. Use it to set up your events and set alerts, so you don't miss anything.

Calendar Views

Select the view you want – by day, week, month, year or list – by tapping the tabs at the top. Each calendar uses a different colour to mark its events, so you can see at a glance when there are busy work periods, for example.

Creating Events

1. In any view, tap the + button, and a new event box appears.

2. Enter a name and location for the event.

3. Tap the **Starts** section to bring up the date and time controls, and enter the details.

4. Select **Repeat** and choose how frequently it reoccurs, then select the calendar to add it to. When finished, tap **Done**.

In all but the year view, you can also tap-and-hold until the new event box appears and then release to open the Add Event box.

Edit Events

Tap the event and then tap the **Edit** button. In week or month view, if you've got the wrong day, just drag the event to a new date.

Search Events

If you know there's something you've been invited to but can't remember the date, search Events. Tap **List** from the top menu bar and then enter the keywords you're looking for in the **Search** box.

Above: Tap the + button to add a new event to your calendar by entering the name, location, time and details.

CONTACTS

Your Contacts app is far more than just a list of names and addresses; it is also your social hub from which you can send an email, text or even Tweet.

IMPORT CONTACTS

If you have your list of contacts elsewhere – in Gmail, webmail or an email program such as Outlook – then you don't want to re-enter them one-by-one. Fortunately, you can import your contacts to iCloud and sync them to your iPad.

Above: Once you have turned Contacts on in your iCloud settings the app will appear in your iCloud Home screen.

1. As iCloud is built into the iPad, all you need to do is to activate it, using your Apple ID. Go to **Settings**, then **iCloud**, and make sure **Contacts** is turned on.

2. On your Mac or PC, go to your existing mail program or webmail account and export all contacts in a single vCard file. How this is done will vary but the program's help file should explain what to do.

3. On your computer, access iCloud in your browser by going to www.icloud.com. Sign in with your Apple ID and password, then select **Contacts**. Click the **Settings** button with its Gear icon that's in the bottom-left, and click **Import vCard**.

4. Browse to where you saved the vCard and select it. This will import the contacts online, which will then be synced to your Contacts address book on the iPad.

Add Contacts Manually

In order to add a contact directly to the iPad, tap the Contacts app to open it, then press the + button. A blank form appears. Enter the details, tapping the return key on the keyboard to move between fields.

Tap the green button beside add field, and there are options to add a contact's nickname, the phonetic pronunciation of their name, birthday, Twitter handle and so on. Tap Done when finished.

Above: Manually add contacts to your iPad by filling in the various details within each Add Field box and tapping Done.

SECURITY

Given the range of all that you can do on the iPad, from your accounts to buying and selling on the web, there are a number of security measures that can help you keep your private information confidential.

PASSWORD PROTECTION

The simplest way of keeping your information private is to use password protection – but there are varying degrees of security to the passcodes you use.

Locking Your iPad – Step-by-Step

1. Go to **Settings**, then tap **General** from the list on the left and scroll down to **Passcode Lock**. If you turn Simple Passcode on, your password will be a four-digit number. Otherwise you can use a longer password, featuring numbers and letters, for extra security.

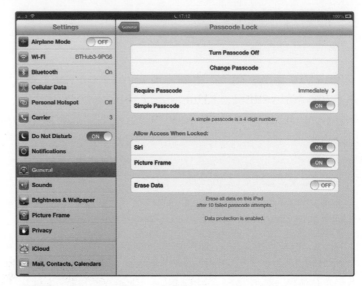

Above: Turn on the passcode option within the general Settings menu to increase iPad security.

2. Tap **Turn Passcode On**. With the Simple Passcode option enter a four-digit number you'll remember and re-enter it when prompted.

3. Select **Require Passcode** and select the interval, from more than four hours to immediately, before the iPad locks. The shorter the interval, the more secure it is.

4. Even when the iPad is locked, there may be certain services you want to use, such as asking Siri to set a Reminder. Under the **Allow Access When Locked** section, choose which apps you want to be available in the background.

Hot Tip

For **Find My iPad** to work, it has to be turned on at all times, which will use some battery power, but it does offer great peace of mind in case anything happens to your iPad.

5. If you turn on **Erase Data**, all information on your iPad is wiped clean after 10 failed attempts to enter the right passcode.

iCloud Security

When your personal information is sent from your iPad to iCloud over the internet, it is encrypted, employing the same level of security as that used by major banks. It is also stored on Apple's servers in an encrypted format. Apple also recommend you use a strong password with your Apple ID that is used for accessing iCloud. It should be a minimum of eight characters and include uppercase and lowercase letters, and a number.

SETTING UP TOUCH ID

The latest iPad Air and iPad Mini models can enable Touch ID to add a unique layer of security. Here's how to set it up:

1. Go to **Settings** then select **Touch ID & Passcode**.

2. Select to add a fingerprint, then follow the instructions to register your fingerprint.

Right: Touch ID allows you to use your fingerprint as a security measure.

3. Once completed you can select to use the fingerprint as the iPad unlock by swiping the iPad Unlock toggle in the Settings.

4. Additionally, you can also assign the fingerprint to authorize iTunes and App Store purchases.

FIND MY iPAD

Whether your iPad has been stolen or you've simply mislaid it, you can track it down, provided you've already set up Find My iPad.

Find Your Device

1. To start tracking your iPad, go to **Settings**, **iCloud** and turn on **Find My iPad**.

2. As soon as you've done this, a permission box opens, asking you to confirm that you are happy for the iPad to be tracked and its location shown on a map. Tap **Allow**.

Above: Turn on Find My iPad in your iCloud settings to ensure it can be tracked via Location Services.

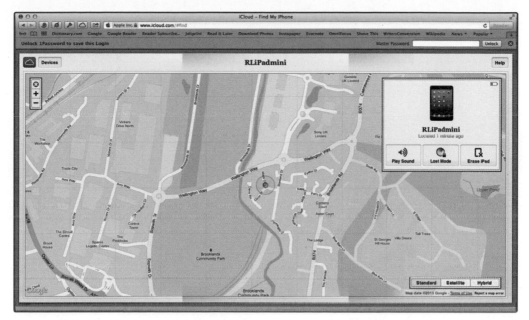

Above: You can choose actions for when your iPad has been tracked, for example playing sounds, locking it remotely and erasing its content.

3. In **Settings**, tap **Privacy** and turn on **Location Services**. Find My iPad should also be turned on.

4. You can download the Find My iPad app (called Find My iPhone) from iTunes and use this on another iDevice, such as iPhone, to track your iPad. Once it's downloaded, log in using your iCloud username and password.

5. Alternatively, you can log in direct through Find My iPhone on the iCloud website. Go to www.icloud.com and use your Apple ID to sign in. Click on **Devices**, and any that can be found are shown with a green pin on the map. Any that can't be located will have a red pin.

6. Click on the pin, and it shows you the last time the iPad was tracked to that address. Click on the information button and a new window opens.

USEFUL APPS

COMMUNICATION

Friendly for Facebook: The full Facebook experience designed specifically for the iPad.

Skype for iPad: Instant message, voice or video call to friends and family around the world.

StumbleUpon: Stumble your way through a creative network of videos, photos and web pages.

Tweetbot: Nice design and lots of ways to customize your Twitter experience.

CONNECTIVITY

Instagram: iPhone version of the fun social network for taking and sharing photos.

iPhoto: Browse, edit and share your photos from the iPad.

PhotoSync: Wirelessly transfers your photos and videos.

TV, MOVIES AND MUSIC VIDEO

Netflix: The subscription service for watching TV and films on your iPad.

Skyfire Web Browser for iPad: The browser that does let you watch Flash videos on the iPad.

YouTube: No longer a built-in app, but you can still get access to one of the world's greatest collections of videos.

BOOKS/NEWS

Flipboard: Your Social News Magazine: Personal magazine combining international news sources and your social networks.

Google Play Books: Provides access to millions of books – free and paid-for.

iBooks: Apple's ebook reader and bookstore.

Zinio: Buy and read magazines on your iPad.

REFERENCE/LIFESTYLE

Epicurious: Recipes for foodies.

HowStuffWorks for iPad: All you need to know.

Weather: Is it cold outside? Find out.

Wikipanion: A faster and easier way to access Wikipedia.

ENTERTAINMENT

Angry Birds: Destroy greedy pigs in a number of environments.

Podcasts: Manage your podcasts.

Spotify: Access millions of songs and listen free or subscribe.

WORK

Dictionary.com: English dictionary and thesaurus for the iPad.

Dropbox: Share and sync your docs, photos and videos.

GoodReader for iPad: Robust, flexible PDF reader.

PrintCentral Pro: Print to all printers (not just AirPrint printers).

SECURITY

1Password: Remember the master password and 1Password remembers the rest.

Find My iPhone: Use another iDevice to find your iPad and protect your data.

INDEX